BEYOND LIGHT AMERICAN LANDSCAPES

Dedicated to the late Cole Weston
and those photographers
who have blazed a path for us to follow—
the ties that bind us together …

ROBERT WERLING

BEYOND LIGHT AMERICAN LANDSCAPES

ROBERT WERLING

MERRELL
LONDON · NEW YORK

FOREWORD
COLE WESTON

The term "straight photography" began with my father, Edward Weston, in Mexico in the early 1920s. This new way of seeing is now called photographic modernism, and my father was at the forefront of this process of change. He used the term "pure" or "straight" photography to mean that which was not manipulated to imitate painting. This was a different approach from that of traditional landscape photographers. As I recall, most landscape photography was pictorial, soft-focus, bent on imitating painting. It was while my father was in Mexico that he made this great shift to sharp focus and full-scale prints. He had his own built-in zone system.[1] He knew instinctively that a one-second exposure would give him a gray dune, so he just bumped it up three times for more density. When he returned to California in 1923, he remained committed to this new direction of straight photography. As he said himself, "for landscape workers, nature unimproved by man is simply chaos, man must isolate and select from her."

My father did much of his best-known work along the California coast, on Point Lobos and in the dunes of Oceano. He was introduced to Gavin Arthur in Oceano and associated with the Dunites in Moy Mell.[2] He was influenced by them and would go there occasionally to live in a cabin for a week or so. He used the dunes as the subject for his landscapes and as background for his nude series with Charis in 1936.[3] Those were Depression years, and we tried to use film as efficiently as possible back then. My brother Brett, on the other hand, would bracket his exposures all over the place and say, "Well, film is cheap." This was totally contrary to Ansel Adams's zone system.

The dunes are very difficult, and to my eye Robert Werling's are very different from Brett's and Edward Weston's. My father's approach to the dunes was more sensual, and he used a longer gray scale. Bob's dunes are often bolder, stranger, and they push the concept of what we may call reality to the limit. My father used long exposures but never experimented with them, whereas Bob uses long exposures to enhance movement, employing it as an abstract element in his pictures.

Many people shy away from beauty in landscape photography because it's too schmaltzy. But I believe in photographic beauty in its own right, provided it affects you in a certain way. It's harder to make something meaningful out of a landscape. Take my father's work, for example. His most meaningful photographs were abstract and detailed. He had the ability to take a straightforward landscape and make something out of it. Getting people to see something in a different way than ever before—that was one of his greatest talents.

We live in landscape country. Western photography is much more open than that of the eastern United States, which is more closed and introspective. True landscapes are rapidly disappearing, all taken up by freeways and crap. There is no new subject matter in the world to photograph, and now, with all this digital adding of stuff here and there, photographers may as well become painters.

Through his association with both Brett Weston and Ansel Adams, Bob learned the power and subtlety a straight photograph could have. With Ansel Adams he learned to use the zone system to control tonality, which is so difficult to achieve, and with Brett he developed the ability to exaggerate it. Fascinated with the quality of my father's prints, Bob began contact-printing his negatives. In contact printing you use the whole image, not just bits and pieces as in enlarging. More discipline is required with large-format work. Bob works with both an 8 × 10 inch (20 × 25 cm) camera and a 14 inch (35.5 cm) commercial Ektar, as my father and I did on Point Lobos with the first Kodachrome

in 1946. Photographers of Bob's generation still want to carry all this big stuff. Nowadays people prefer to stay home and do it digitally. To me, the visual thing is the most important, and with the 8 × 10 view you see exactly what you are going to get. You don't have to think about enlarging it. The 4 × 5 inch (10 × 12.5 cm) format is good, but with 8 × 10 you get a whole different impact. You get swept into it, into the ultimate.

There have been so many images made that it's difficult today for any photographer to do something different. Bob sees it with his own heart and eyes. It's amazing, though, how people can look at the same thing but see it differently. I remember the day when, quite by accident, my father and I photographed the same rock. I was concerned about being compared to him, but he just said, "Don't worry about it, Cole. I like yours better."

Bob's love for the art of photography has grown and matured steadily. While his work is in the realm of Brett Weston, he has his own personal way of seeing. Bob's black-and-white images are powerful. He uses black intensely, not as subject but as shape. What is familiar to the average eye is abstracted to the point where it is not readily discernible without

considerable concentration. His work presents a bold direction, a completely new dimension.

Part of the satisfaction of being a teacher is to see students develop and realize their own innate gift, watching them learn to see and grow as Bob has done. It's a real delight to see his work presented in these fine reprints, which accurately reproduce the quality of his photographs.

Bob represents yet another generation that has pushed the traditions of the past to the next level. For him, photography is more than just traveling and recording images. Photography has been a way of life for my family, and it is no less for Bob Werling.

The text is based on an interview with Cole Weston before his death in 2003.

Notes
1 For a definition of the term "zone system," see p. 20, note 5.
2 See p.114.
3 Charis Wilson, whom Edward Weston married in 1938.

THROUGH MY EYES
ROBERT WERLING

Generations ago, wilderness and the land were something to fear, conquer, and inhabit, and later sell at a profit. Now there is scarcely a landscape that has not had a footprint laid to it. However, there seems to be something in the American spirit that cries out, "Don't fence me in, leave me alone, let me discover and experience it for myself!"

Whenever we encounter a beautiful scene we seem to want to record it and share our sense of wonder. What we feel deeply is often difficult to put into words, and many photographs are just records of a time or experience. This leads us to the question of photography and reality. Is a photograph real or does it merely inform? Usually, the more information there is and, above all, the more tones there are, the closer we approach reality. Since the objects we photograph exist in the real world, we need to make some sort of departure in order to present subjects in a more poetic way. One doesn't look at something for what it is, but rather for what it could become.

Photographs are not realistic in the usual sense but rather departures from reality. Skies can be blackened, shadows made empty, movement exaggerated, and textures enhanced. These characteristics exist only in the world of photography, of film and technique. Black and white is itself a departure from our world of color, and perhaps music, more than any other form of expression, is most closely related to black-and-white photography, in that it lends itself to abstract thinking. It is difficult not to make a cliché from certain spectacular land formations in the West, but instead we should aim to revisualize them in a different, personal way. To make an abstract out of nature is ordinarily, to use Ansel Adams's words, "to make a photographic extract." We are simply not used to looking at something closely and intensely for any length of time. Adams and Edwin Land helped pioneer the first instant photography, the Polaroid process. By the 1980s Adams knew already that the new direction in photography would be with electronics and that it would offer new means and techniques for creative expression unimaginable at that time. However, these new techniques don't help create more insightful photographs unless they are used with imagination by the photographer. Ansel Adams once said, "It's amazing how photography has advanced without progressing."

Soon does the new become the old in our rapidly changing society. That which was radical becomes acceptable. Change and the desire to communicate at increasing technological speed represent the norm in today's impatient world. Soon film, chemicals, and quality silver-emulsion papers will disappear into the past, giving further meaning to the term "vintage print." The landscape, perhaps more than any other subject for photography, requires patience and a sensitivity that goes beyond light. To be constantly observing, to be there, to experience and record and later present to a viewer that which, in some mysterious way, connects to our lives … to me, that's photography.

TRADITION, VISION, AND "INNER SIGHT": ROBERT WERLING'S LANDSCAPE PHOTOGRAPHY
SIMONE KLEIN

"Vision, sensitivity, an understanding of life, these are all necessary tools for those who would create something universal through the camera lens, something universal that is part of an organic whole, that fulfills certain functions within this whole, that is pure natural form; perhaps only a fragment, but one that reveals or symbolizes the rhythms of life."

EDWARD WESTON[1]

"I think photography has contributed tremendously to developing one of our most important senses, our inner sight … . Capturing an image on film is a way of expressing what and how I see and feel. Photography, as other forms of art, is a license to speak one's mind, and photographs speak a universal language that everyone can understand."

ROBERT WERLING[2]

The photographs of Californian Robert Werling belong to the tradition of photographic chronicles of the magnificent and diverse nature of the American West Coast. In terms of motifs and technical precision, they call to mind the works of several noteworthy predecessors: Carleton E. Watkins, Eadweard Muybridge, William Henry Jackson, Ansel Adams, Edward Weston, and Brett Weston. Common to all of these artists is a detached, almost contemplative affirmation of an intact, sublime order in which the human being is a subordinate part of a great whole.

Werling's nature photography both follows and transcends this tradition. Like every photograph, his images are interpretations of the visual reality that surrounds us. In his choice of motifs, the composition of his images, and the scale of tonal values that can be influenced by the photographer during the printing process, he shapes the visual effect of the photograph and shifts perception of this one segment of reality in the direction he has chosen. The objective view of nature we recognize in nineteenth-century photographs gives way to a subjectively molded, individually graspable sense of nature. Stylistically speaking, the specific quality of Werling's

landscape photography is abstraction; in terms of interpretation, it is contemplation. He creates images of an "inner sight" which transform the manifestations of nature into internalized, personalized, yet universally valid landscapes.

Robert Werling was born in San Francisco in 1946. His interest in art emerged during early childhood. He was particularly intrigued by the absence of color in ink and pencil drawings. After finishing art school in San Francisco, where he acquired basic skills in black-and-white photography, he worked for a while as an illustrator.

He first encountered photographs by Ansel Adams in 1965—8 × 10 inch (20 × 25 cm) black-and-white contact prints of landscape photographs exhibited at the Yosemite Gallery. This experience had a decisive impact on his own development as a photographer. Werling's early contact with the old master, who lived in Carmel, California, grew into a close and amiable teacher–student relationship. Under Adams's tutelage, from 1966 Werling devoted himself exclusively to black-and-white photography. His work was exhibited for the first time at a group exhibition organized in 1969 by the Friends of Photography at Adams's gallery in Carmel.

Werling earned a Bachelor of Arts degree in art photography at the Brooks Institute of Photography in Santa Barbara, California, in 1971. He then worked for some time as an architecture and product photographer. During this period his independent work was shown at a number of exhibitions.

His close collaboration with Ansel Adams over many years formed the foundation for Werling's career as an artist. During that period he perfected his darkroom technique, painstakingly applying Adams's "zone system" in his own work, photographed primarily with a large-frame camera in keeping with the model established by the group f/64, and discovered many of his motifs during photographic explorations with the master. Werling's early photographs (1966–71) clearly reflect Adams's influence in their prominent, fine progressions of gray, their precisely detailed motifs, and their atmospheric or dramatized rendering of nature.

Trained as a pianist, Ansel Adams (born 1902 in San Francisco, died 1984 in Carmel), who had taken up amateur photography in his youth, began his career as a professional photographer in 1930 after having seen the purist light-images of Paul Strand. In 1932 he joined Edward Weston, Imogen Cunningham,

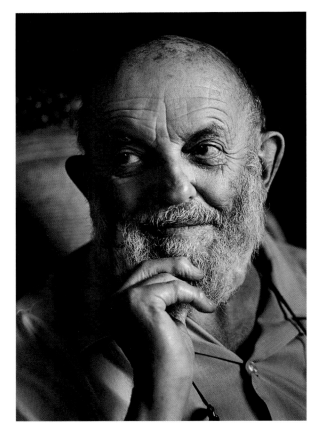

FAR LEFT
Ansel Adams, Carmel, California, 1980
Photographed by Robert Werling

LEFT
Imogen Cunningham, San Francisco, California, 1972
Photographed by Robert Werling

Willard Van Dyke, Sonia Noskowiak, John Paul Edwards, and the wealthy amateur photographer Henry Swift in founding the group f/64.[3] In the spirit of "straight" photography propagated by Paul Strand and Alfred Stieglitz, these artists demanded absolute authenticity of depiction and sharp precision in the photographic image. They categorically rejected soft focus and blurred contours, along with all forms of print manipulation of the kind commonly employed by pictorialist photographers around the turn of the century.

The name of the group is derived from a diaphragm number of the photographic lens. It signifies to a large extent the qualities of clearness and definition of the photographic image, which is an important element in the work of members of this group ... . The members of group f/64 believe that photography, as an art form, must develop along lines defined by the actualities and limitations of the photographic medium, and must always remain independent of ideological conventions of art and aesthetics that are reminiscent of a period and culture antedating the growth of the medium itself.[4]

The members of the group, which remained intact until 1935, preferred the 8 × 10 inch, large-format camera for most of their photographic work. Ansel Adams articulated these demanding requirements with respect to technique and print quality on a number of occasions, initially in his first textbook, *Making a Photograph* (1935), and from 1946 as an instructor at the California School of Fine Arts in San Francisco and the co-founder, with Beaumont Newhall and David McAlpin, of the Photography Department of the Museum of Modern Art in New York. During the 1930s he developed the zone system, a light-measurement process based upon Edward Weston's "previsualization" technique, which served as an aid to the photographer in calculating gradations of the gray scale in the finished print.[5] Adams defined the procedure as follows in 1943:

Seeing and visualizing is the fundamental prerequisite, of course. A photograph is not a coincidence, it is a concept. It exists at or just before the moment of exposure. From this moment on, until the print is finished, everything depends upon technical skill. The previsualized photograph becomes a finished print through a series of processes that are unique to the medium. Alterations and additions can be made during these processes, of course, but the essential image of what has been "seen" undergoes no further significant change.[6]

By virtue of their traditionalism and their visual qualities, Adams's photographs of the Yosemite Valley and the American West are masterpieces of landscape photography. "In a time when the pattern of creative statement has favored the personal, the oblique, the esoteric, and the scarce, Adams's work has been epic, frontal, popular, and prolific. ... At its best—intense, extroverted, and heroic—Adams's is a major vision."[7] Or: "Adams's own photographs are interpretations of light, texture, place, and mood, always produced within the ultimate clarity of detail and tonal values. An ardent conservationist, he finds a blade of grass, a charred stump, the movement of water as consequential as the lofty grandeur of a mountain range or the vast space of valleys and lakes. His images are an affirmation of the enduring relationship of man and nature."[8]

During those years, the late 1960s, the young Werling met a number of prominent personalities from the West Coast photography scene, many of whom were frequent visitors at Ansel Adams's home in Carmel—the curators and art historians Beaumont and Nancy Newhall, the photographers Imogen Cunningham, Brett Weston, and Cole Weston, and many of Adams's students. Werling's encounters and discussions with these people represented a constant source of inspiration

Robert Werling, Santa Barbara, California, 1995
Photographed by Wolfgang Bartels

and promoted the further development of his own work.

Through the intercession of Imogen Cunningham, he received his first commercial photo commission, from the University of California in Berkeley (1971), which enabled him to take his first long journey. He traveled to Japan, where he spent more than a year, doing landscape and portrait photography. His experience of the country and its traditions, which he recorded with his camera in landscapes and portraits, brought him another step further in his work. Werling's Japanese landscapes, in particular, already show evidence of the use of a stylistic tool that would later become increasingly characteristic of his work: abstraction. This involved, on the one hand, subtle gradations of gray, which Werling, inspired by Japanese ink paintings (*Sumi-e*), sought to translate in his photographs; and, on the other, the graphic accentuation of specific elements of the photograph through the use of strong contrasts.[9] The resulting landscape is no longer merely a positivistic rendering of a section of the whole: it is a pointedly selected, personalized individual image, a single impression filtered from the grand drama of nature and interpreted through photographic technique.

Werling's close friendship with Brett Weston also influenced his photography in important ways. From 1975 they often traveled and worked together, photographing side by side in Hawaii and along the coast of California.

Brett Weston (born 1911 in Los Angeles, died 1993 in Hawaii), the second son of Edward Weston, learned to photograph as a fourteen-year-old in Mexico under his father's guidance. Departing from the sensual, poetic, highly symbolic style of Edward Weston, his own photographic style soon took form in a more abstract, reductive, vigorous approach to the representation of nature.

Brett Weston's photographs gained international attention in exhibitions and publications in the late 1920s. In 1929 eight of his works were presented at *Film und Foto*, an exhibition of the Deutscher Werkbund in Stuttgart, along with photographs by his fellow Americans Edward Weston, Edward Steichen (these two photographers organized the American section of the show), Imogen Cunningham, Berenice Abbott, Paul Outerbridge, Ralph Steiner, and Charles Sheeler. His picture *Tin Roof, Mexico* (1926) was reproduced in Franz Roh's and Jan Tschichold's book *Foto-Auge* (1929), the most important

critical guide to European and American avant-garde photography of the 1920s. Brett Weston, who had worked with his father as a commercial portrait photographer since 1927, opened his own studio in Carmel in 1930. The first major retrospective of his work was presented at the M.H. De Young Memorial Museum in San Francisco in 1932. Brett Weston was only twenty-one years old at the time.

From the 1950s his photographs became increasingly abstract: landscape details, formal reduction to recurring, twisting, or geometrically intertwining elements whose surfaces are almost palpable on the photographic paper. "We are allowed in these pictures to be in two places at one time, that is, in the domain of the rational mind and in the realm of timeless imagination … . In such remarkable images [Oceano Dunes, ed.], Brett achieved a synthesis of reality and dour fantasy."[10]

Brett Weston lived and worked in Carmel until his death. He is now regarded as one of the great masters of classical American landscape photography. His influence on Werling's work is evident in motifs in which the scenic context of the comprehensive view of nature is abandoned and nature is represented in fragmentary form: Leaves in the morning dew

appear as a full-surface relief with variations on recurring geometric forms; their texture has an almost tactile quality. "Brett seemed to be able to combine power of design with subtlety of tone in his work. It was this departure from classical composition that caused me to explore the abstract in natural found objects. Brett Weston was not only my friend and teacher. He was also a profound inspiration."[11]

In 1984 Werling began making new prints from original negatives made by Marion Post Wolcott during her years of work for the Farm Security Administration (FSA) in the 1930s and 1940s. He printed under Wolcott's guidance, and this work with her negatives, combined with Wolcott's critical appraisal of his prints, posed a major challenge for Werling, who had already gained acclaim as an outstanding black-and-white printer. During this period of mutual and often very critical concern with Wolcott's material that documents an important part of American social history, which continued until Marion Post Wolcott's death in 1990, an unusually close friendship developed between these two photographers whose subjects and working methods differed so greatly.

Traveling and photographing nature in its great diversity at different locations has always

been a driving impulse and a constant source of renewed inspiration for Werling. The photographs taken during his travels in Alaska in 1981—numerous mountain panoramas, images of glaciers and formations of snow and ice—are profoundly contemplative images of a strange, inaccessible world, many of them exhibiting a quality of respectful distance and awe.

Werling has made regular trips to Europe, frequently to Germany, since 1985. His photographs of European landscapes expose the signs of human intervention—in mountain scenes with paths and buildings and in urban landscapes. As in his images of diverse American landscapes in California—the Sierra Nevada, Yosemite, the coastline—Hawaii, or Arizona, he captures the specific essence of nature in these photographs and translates it into a larger, universal context. The individual image becomes a part of a great whole. Together, all of the photographs form a panorama of nature *per se*.

The tradition of landscape photography of the American West, and thus the roots of Werling's art, took shape during the nineteenth century. Concurrent with the geological exploration of this part of the North American continent and its exploitation by commerce

and tourism, images of the natural monuments and native inhabitants of the region were recorded with the aid of the new medium of photography. Photographic technology now made it possible to transport even large glass negatives on expeditions and to make prints on a monumental scale. Thus the earliest photographs are documents of a new mode of seeing and experiencing life, of the discovery of a new living space, of pride in the "new land" and respect for its grandeur.

Timothy O'Sullivan (1840–82), who began his career as a war photographer and produced dramatic images of the American Civil War, accompanied a number of expeditions between 1867 and 1874 and was the first photographer to compile a comprehensive picture of the West, its landscapes, and its ancient cultures. William Henry Jackson (1843–1942), a professional landscape and portrait photographer active from the 1870s to the turn of the century, accompanied the first expedition of the US Geological Survey of the Territories into the Yellowstone region in 1871. He became one of the most highly acclaimed landscape photographers of the American West. The Californian landscape, and particularly the Yosemite Valley, provided numerous motifs

Cole Weston, Garrapata Beach, California, 1982
Photographed by Robert Werling

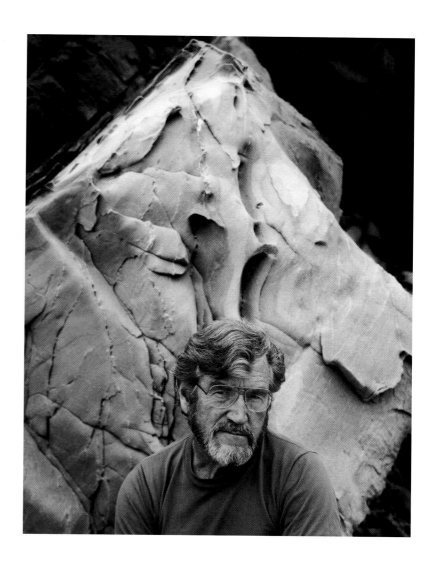

for photographers beginning in the Gold Rush years of the mid-1850s. Carleton E. Watkins (1820–1916) and Eadweard Muybridge (1830–1904) were famous chroniclers of the spectacular landscapes of northern California. Their albumen prints, many of which were larger than 15 × 20 inches (38 × 50 cm), are oversized, multi-faceted records of the diversity, vitality, and drama of the landscape. In an approach much like that used by the French photographer Gustave Le Gray in his seascapes and harbor photographs made near Le Havre and Sète (c. 1856), Muybridge used two negatives and copied moving cloud formations into the print in order to dramatize his images of the landscape.

These early photographs of the West exhibit a high level of technical quality and a pictorial structure reminiscent of classical paintings. Their colors are reduced to the tonal values of the prints—albumen prints, in most cases, with chocolate or sepia-brown tonal gradations, made from collodion negatives—yet these photographic landscapes are staged compositions. Such details as bizarre rock formations or giant trees were extracted, while larger contexts such as rivers, waterfalls, or canyons were rendered as magnificent backdrops. Photographers strived for maximum naturalism,

but each photographer's personal "signature" is evident in, for example, the choice of camera perspective or the composition of a given picture, despite the abundance of information and the desire to document in a universally comprehensible form. The photographs made during this period are characterized by optical richness, an overpowering spatial reach, tonal subtleness, and visual energy and intensity. They are regarded today as masterpieces of the history of landscape photography.[12]

Impressionist or pictorial photography of the late nineteenth and early twentieth centuries, which influenced popular taste in art photography in America until well into the 1920s, appears to have found little of interest in West Coast motifs. The naturalist tradition, which consistently realized new landscape discoveries in literal images, was taken up and pursued in the early twentieth century in the classicism of Ansel Adams and the Modernism of Edward and Brett Weston and the f/64 group. Photographers such as Wynn Bullock (1902–75) and Minor White (1908–76), representing another generation of West Coast photography, introduced during the latter half of the twentieth century new aspects into nature photography in terms of technique and form and of reception and interpretation.

These aspects have often been described as manifestations of mysticism or spirituality.

In his own work Werling practices the aesthetics of the New Vision, conceived by Edward Weston, embodied in the work of Ansel Adams, and pursued to its extreme in the "abstract realism" of Brett Weston. Werling, who learned his craft before developing his artistic position, has articulated his own unique approach to nature in his photographs since the 1980s. In complete command of his technical resources—his camera; his own method of previsualization, which is not strictly based upon the historical model; his favored large-format negatives; and the perfection he achieves in printing—he expresses his own personal, emotional response to the motifs he finds. His clear, richly contrastive presentation removes the motif from its local context. The landscape detail becomes a hypernaturalistic experiment in form and pattern in which motion and stasis collide in defiance of logic, and thus unnaturally, and perspective is altered. The natural manifestation metamorphoses into an abstract, tactile, and rhythmic interplay of forms.

A comparison of what is perhaps Werling's most powerful group of works, the images of Oceano Dunes, a place that has fascinated him since the very beginning of his career, with the photographs Edward Weston made at the same location in 1936–37 and then with Brett Weston's dune photographs from the 1930s and later, reveals striking differences. Edward Weston's images are fine-limbed, sensual in their most delicate gradations of gray and the smooth, associative elegance of their lines. In contrast, Brett Weston's interpretation of the diverse dune landscape appears unfiltered, immediate, rather more masculine than feminine, expressive. Werling takes this reductive approach a step further. The dark areas of his photographs have few or no interior lines or patterns. They are integrated within the image as isolated accents, as pure form. Hill formations, horizon lines, and fine ripples in the sand also appear as institutionalized forms, as if precisely drawn with an ink brush, yet devoid of all causality. In these photographs the act of viewing the landscape becomes an act of contemplation, a personal inner journey, the opening of an "inner sight." This romantic sensitivity to nature is a characteristic of Werling's photographs that transcends the tradition of West Coast photography.

Notes

1 Translated from Edward Weston, "Amerika und Fotografie," in *Film und Foto, Internationale Ausstellung des Deutschen Werkbundes*, Stuttgart 1929; reprinted 1979, ed. Karl Steinorth, p. 13.

2 *Robert Werling: A Way of Seeing*, Santa Barbara 1997, n.p.

3 f/64 stands for aperture setting 64, a setting that allows considerable depth of field and was commonly used with lenses in large-format cameras. Cf. Nancy Newhall, *Ansel Adams, The Eloquent Light*, San Francisco 1973, pp. 74–80.

4 Ansel Adams and Mary Street Alinder (ed.), *Ansel Adams, An Autobiography*, Boston 1985, p. 112.

5 One of the many definitions of the zone system reads as follows: "A framework for understanding exposure and development, and visualizing their effect in advance. Areas of different luminance in the subject are each related to exposure *zones*, and these in turn to approximate *values* of gray in the final print. Thus careful exposure and development procedures permit the photographer to control the negative densities and corresponding print values that will represent specific subject areas, in accordance with the visualized final image." Ansel Adams, *Examples. The Making of 40 Photographs*, Boston 1983, p. 177.

6 Translated from Ansel Adams, "Ein persönliches Credo" (1943), reprinted in edited and abridged form in Wolfgang Kemp, *Theorie der Fotografie III, 1945–1980*, Munich 1999, p. 45. The original essay was published in the *American Annual of Photography for 1944*, pp. 7–16.

7 John Szarkowski (ed.), *The Photographer and the American Landscape*, New York 1963, exhib. cat., The Museum of Modern Art, New York, p. 5.

8 Robert Doty (ed.), *Photography in America from 1841 to Today*, New York 1986, exhib. cat., Whitney Museum of American Art, New York, p. 17.

9 A new style of Japanese painting, based in part on the Chinese ink painting of the Song and Yüan period, which emerged in the fifteenth century in the work of its master, Sesshu, under the influence of Zen, in opposition to the aesthetic, decorative *Yamato-e* style.

10 Van Deren Coke, *Brett Weston, Master Photographer*, Carmel 1989, n.p.

11 *Robert Werling: A Way of Seeing*, Santa Barbara 1997, n.p.

12 For an extensive historical discussion of American landscape photography, see Martin Christadler, "Amerikanische Landschaft: Geologie und Heilsgeschichte, Markt und Manifest Destiny," in *Gustave Le Gray, Carleton E. Watkins. Pioniere der Landschaftsphotographie*, Mainz 1993, exhib. cat., Frankfurt am Main, pp. 107–27.

PLATES

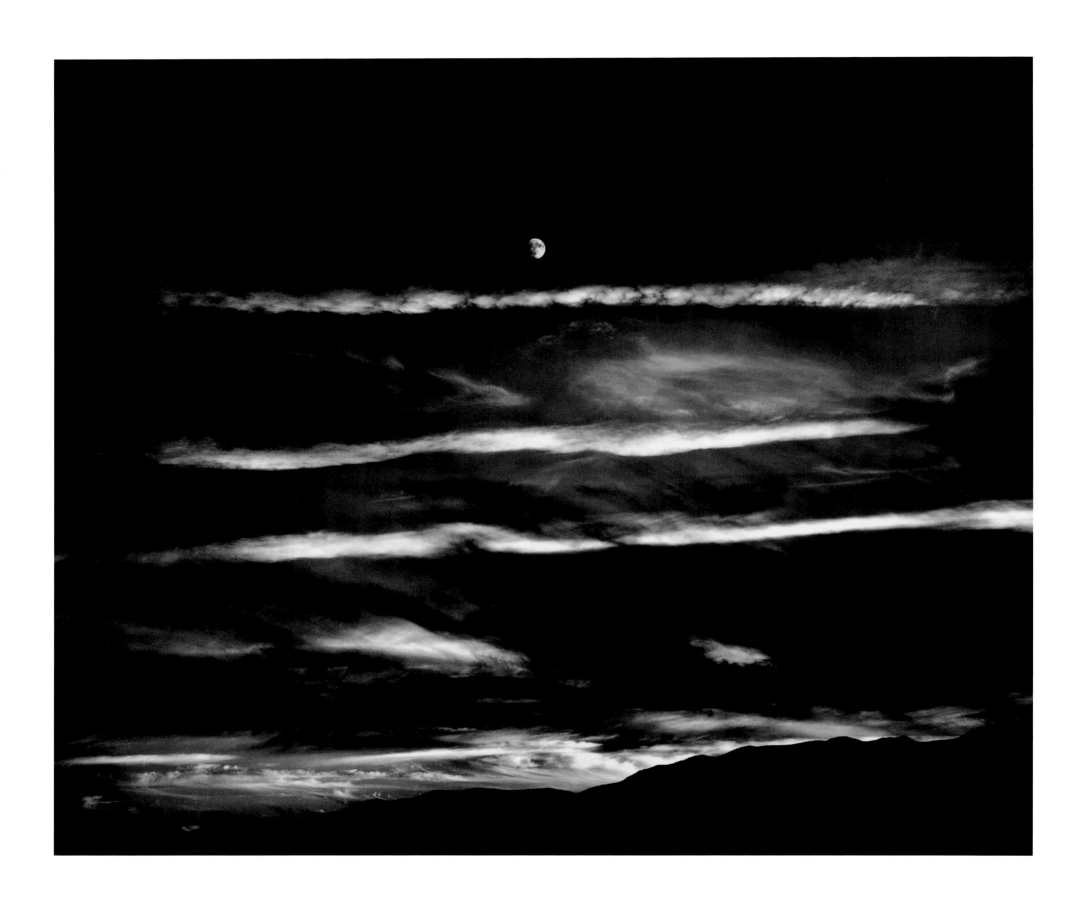

Eastern Sierra Nevada, California, 1976

Clouds, Pacific Coast, 2000

Haliakala, Hawaii, 1985

Oceano Dunes, California, 1990

Three Brothers, Yosemite, California, 1975

Yosemite Valley, California, 1976

Thunderstorm, Canada, 1974

Big Sur, California, 1990

Mono Lake, California, 1979

Sunrise, Death Valley, California, 1986

Saguaro and Moon, Arizona, 1983

Mono Lake, California, 1986

Alabama Hills, Eastern Sierra Nevada, California, 1980

Mount McKinley, Alaska, 1981

High Sierra, California, 1979

Blowing Snow, Yosemite, California, 1976

Eastern Sierra Nevada, California, 1996

Alaska, 1981

Matanuska Glacier, Alaska, 1981

Eastern Sierra Nevada, California, 1980

Portage Glacier, Alaska, 1981

Portage Glacier, Alaska, 1981

San Simeon Coast, California, 1967

Big Sur Coast, California, 2000

Pacific Coast, Trinidad, California, 1999

Pescadero, California, 1971

Mono Lake, California, 1980

Moonstone Beach, Cambria, California, 1998

Big Sur, California, 1999

Rocks and Moss, Moonstone Beach, Cambria, California, 1998

Moonstone Beach, Cambria, California, 1992

Moonstone Beach, Cambria, California, 1994

Moonstone Beach, Cambria, California, 1989

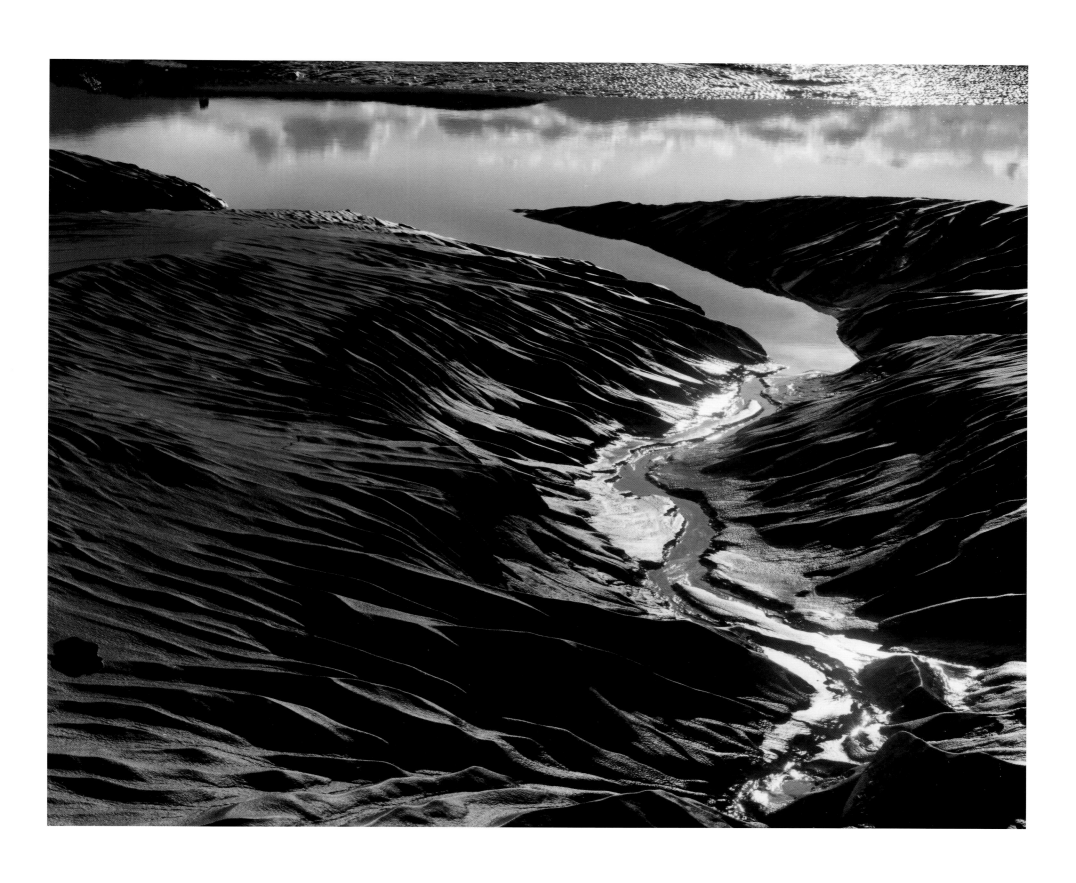

Turnagain Arm, Alaska, 1981

Moonstone Beach, Cambria, California, 1992

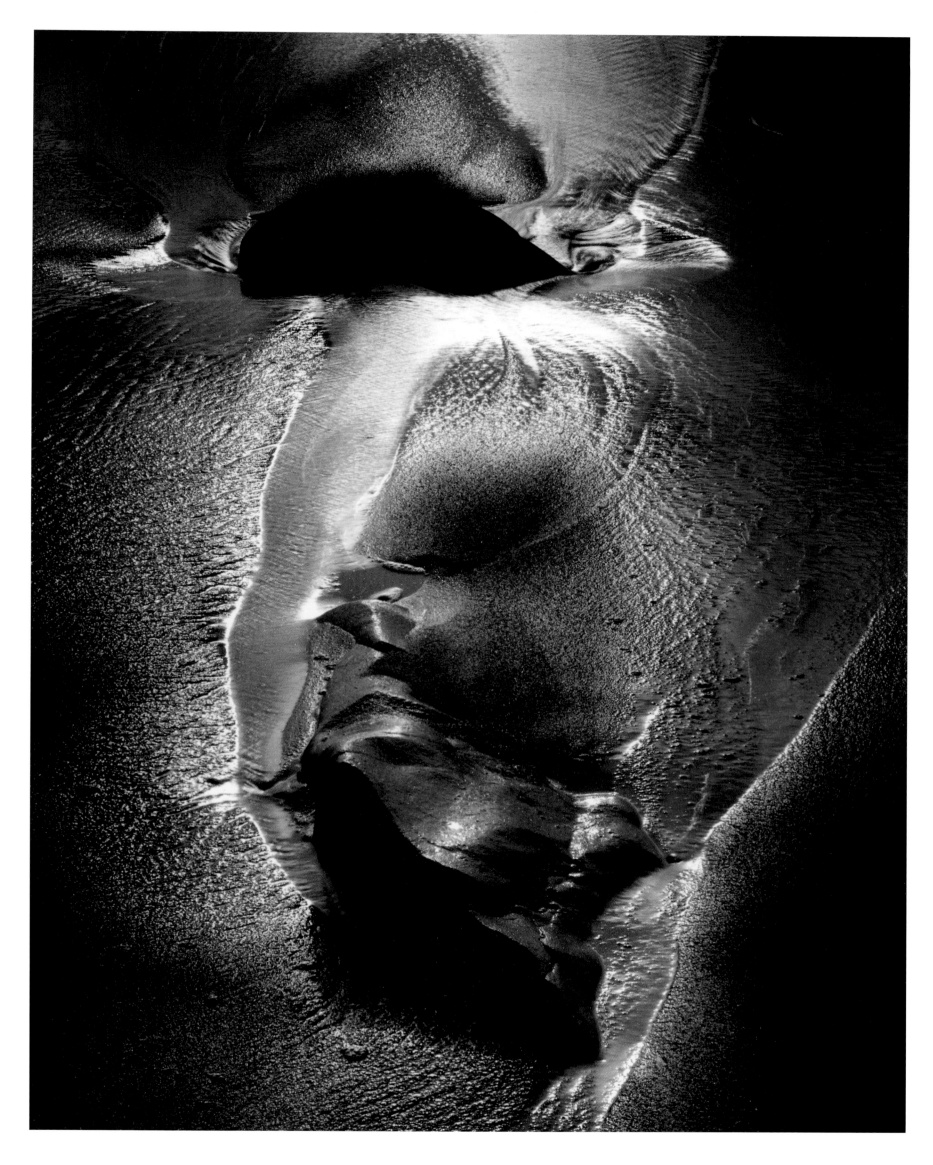

Moonstone Beach, Cambria, California, 1993

Moonstone Beach, Cambria, California, 2001

Ice, Yosemite, California, 1977

Pacific Coast, Big Sur, California, 2001

Kelp, Cambria, California, 1991

Ice, Yosemite, California, 1981

Bridalveil Falls, Yosemite, California, 1976

Ribbon Falls, Alaska, 1981

Frozen Leaves, Alaska, 1981

Frozen Plants, Alaska, 1981

Rope Lava, Hawaii, 1985

Anzo Borego Desert, California, 1980

Eastern Sierra Nevada, California, 1986

Pines, Carmel, California, 1975

Pfeiffer Beach, Big Sur, California, 1988

Pond, Hawaii, 1984

Portage Glacier, Alaska, 1981

Woods, North Carolina, 1984

Lake Merced, San Francisco, California, 1975

Pond, Oregon, 1980

Autumn, Eastern Sierra Nevada, California, 1977

Fairbanks, Alaska, 1981

Forest, Hawaii, 1986

Sutro Forest, San Francisco, California, 1975

Pines, Alaska, 1988

Birch Grove, Alaska, 1981

Winter, Yosemite, California, 1984

Oaks in Snow, Yosemite, California, 1986

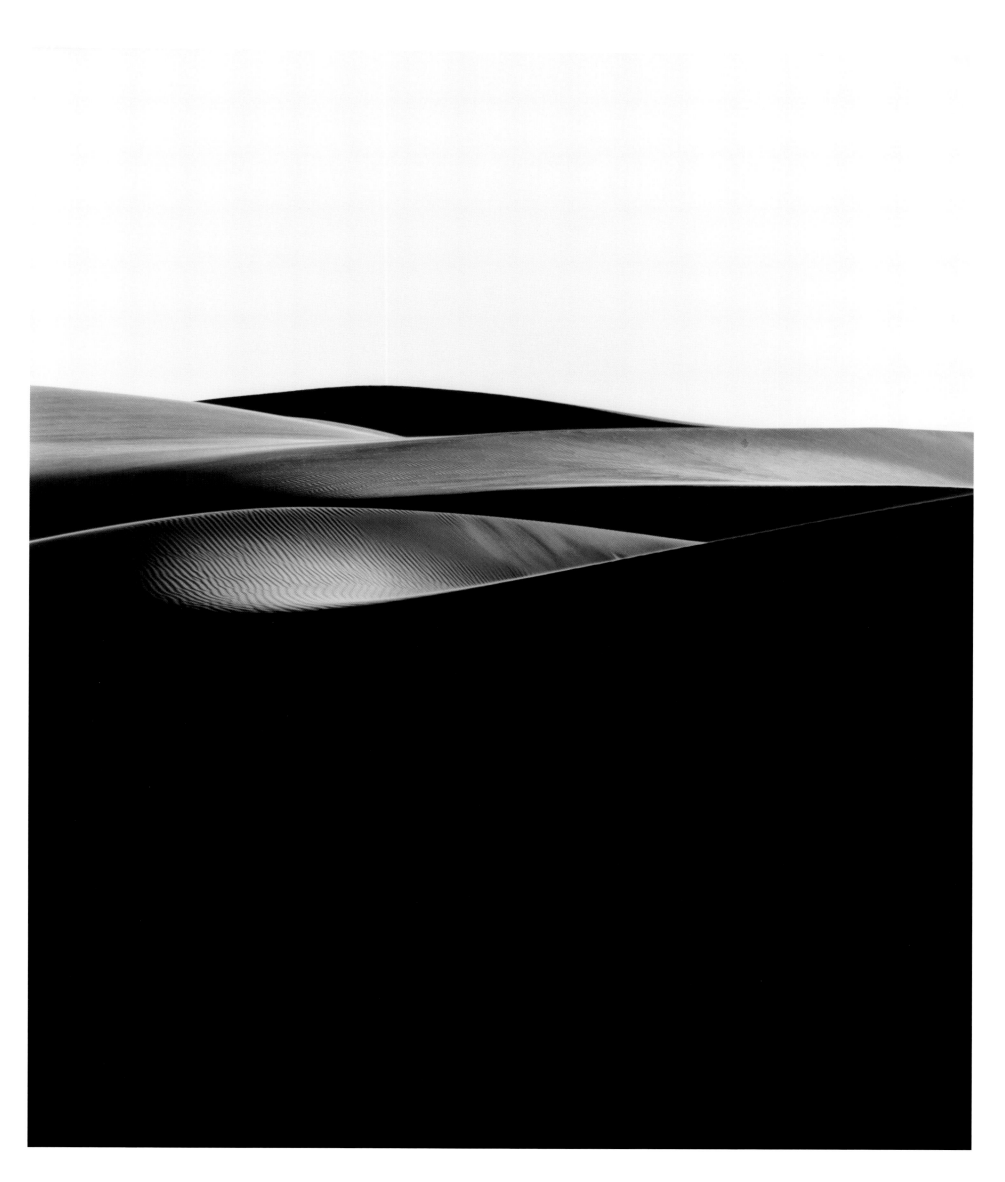

Oceano Dunes, California, 2004

Oceano Dunes, California, 1994

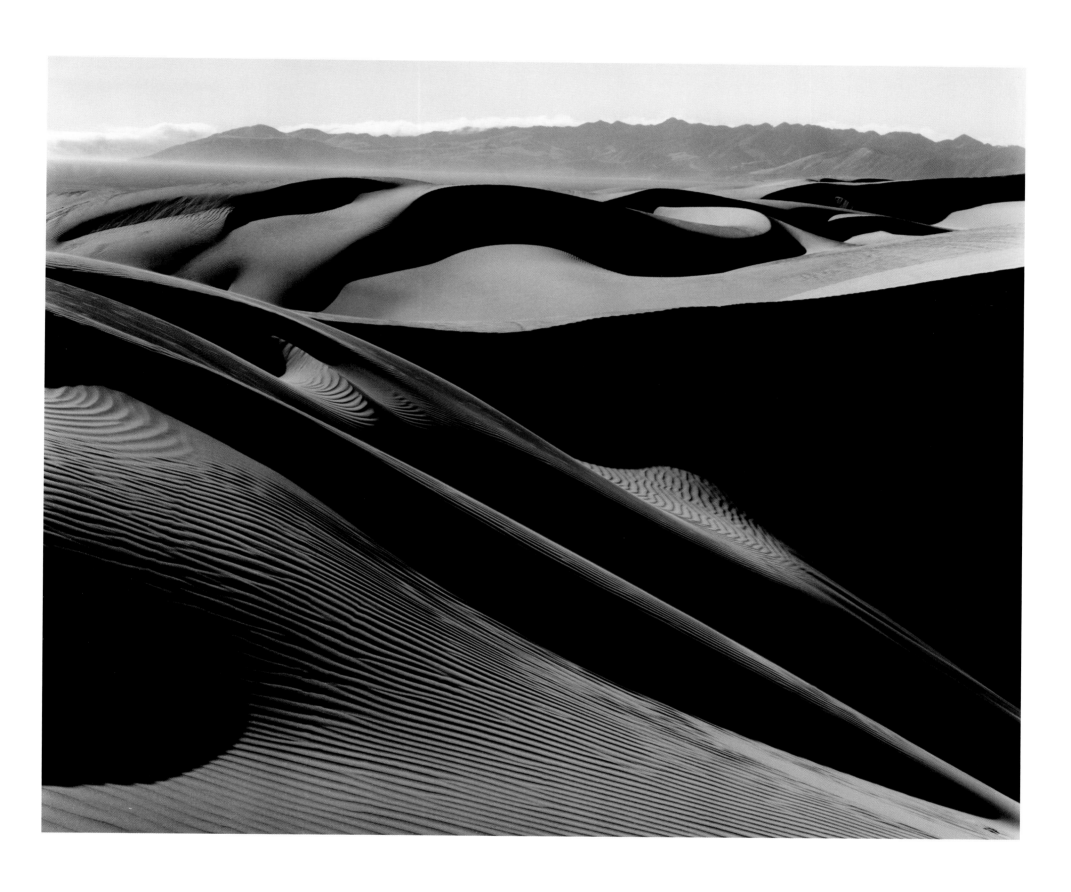

Oceano Dunes, California, 2000

Oceano Dunes, California, 2004

Oceano Dunes, California, 2004

Oceano Dunes, California, 1994

Oceano Dunes, California, 2003

Oceano Dunes, Californa, 1994

Oceano Dunes, California, 1990

Oceano Dunes, California, 1990

Oceano Dunes, California, 1993

Oceano Dunes, California, 1996

Oceano Dunes, California, 1994

Oceano Dunes, California, 1999

THE DUNES AND THE DUNITES
ELIZABETH SCOTT-GRAHAM

The Guadalupe-Nipomo Dunes in California comprise one of the largest, most biodiverse coastal dune ecosystems on earth. The subject of numerous photographs, the dunes are rich not only in biodiversity but also in human and artistic history.

Travelers must come on foot, making their own paths, as though no one had ever walked here before. There are no paths, there are no footprints to follow; you are in a wilderness of light and sculpture untouched by the hand of man, yet available to anyone who chooses to wander here experiencing the sensual excitement of the natural rhythms of the place. The dunes have long attracted seekers of solitude, serene beauty, wilderness, and isolation. The Native American Chumash tribe lived an idyllic life replete with all they needed to thrive. Hundreds of years after their demise, another "tribe" of utopians found inspiration in this landscape.

In 1931, at the height of the Depression, a group of artists, led by Gavin Arthur, the grandson of Chester Alan Arthur, the twenty-first President of the United States of America, established a community of painters, poets, and writers in the dunes. They called themselves the Dunites and for a short time published a literary magazine, *The Dunes Forum*. They built simple cabins, a communal kitchen, dining room, and meeting center, sharing their artistic works and astrology charts and living with a sense of freedom seldom experienced today.

One night Elwood Decker, a Dunite artist who resided in the dunes for many years, was walking down the beach on his way back to his cabin in the dunes. It was high tide and the stars were intensely bright and reflected up at him from the water. "It was an exhilarating physical experience," he wrote; "... being saturated with starlight ... from the billions and billions of stars ahead, behind, above *and* below ... the experience stayed with me for days. I was alive in the light somehow ... at *home* ... the mind ... allowed the sense of sight to divide the scene basically into light and darkness."

Photography is about the tension between light and dark, and the dunes are the perfect subject to play with this tension. What draws Robert Werling back to the dunes is the challenge that he will never get to photograph this particular living dune sculpture again. Because, unlike other, better known American landscapes such as Yosemite, the Grand Canyon, Bryce, or Zion, this is an aeolian landscape. The wind is the sculptor, and only the photographer has the power to preserve the ephemeral landscape. It is the photographer, seeing a basic shape forming in the shadow of a dune, projecting the path of the light and the eventual shape of that shadow, who then captures this singular moment in time and space.

Unlike earlier photographers who photographed on only a few occasions in the dunes, Robert Werling returns again and again. The play of light and dark in his dune landscapes is also harder, bolder, and more abstract, and yet more "of the place" at the same time. As one who has wandered in this wilderness for over thirty years, I find his photographs capture it for the spiritual and inspirational home it will always be to those of us blessed to experience it over and over. It is with exuberant enthusiasm that I see the images of this much-beloved landscape published for the rest of the world to see.

ROBERT WERLING: LIST OF EXHIBITIONS

1971
The Hooker Gallery, Cate School, Carpinteria, California

1973
Santa Barbara Museum of Natural History, Santa
    Barbara, California
Tressidder Union, Stanford University,
    Stanford, California

1974
Pentax Camera Museum, Tokyo, Japan

1977
Brooks Institute of Photography Gallery, Santa Barbara,
    California

1978
Erickson Gallery, Palo Alto, California

1981
Olive Hyde Art Gallery, Fremont, California
Western States Museum at Brooks Institute of
    Photography, Santa Barbara, California
The Broadway Gallery Mall, Los Angeles, California
Robert Werling: Photographs, Anthro Graphics Gallery,
    Hermosa Beach, California

1982
Townsend Room, Santa Barbara Public Library, Santa
    Barbara, California

1983
Ewerts Gallery, Santa Clara, California

1985
Photogalerie: The Compagnie, Hamburg, Germany
Centre pour l'image contemporaine Saint-Gervais,
    Geneva, Switzerland

1987
Artwatch, Santa Barbara, California
Tressidder Union, Stanford University, Stanford,
    California

1988
The University Club of Los Angeles, Los Angeles,
    California

1989
Grauwert Galerie, Hamburg, Germany

1990
Robert Werling: New Work, Grauwert Galerie, Hamburg,
    Germany
New England Photographic Workshop Gallery,
    New Milford, Connecticut

1991
Grauwert Galerie, Hamburg, Germany
Allen Street Gallery, Dallas, Texas

1999
Haus der Fotografie, Hanover, Germany
A Thirty Year Retrospective, Carnegie Art Museum,
    Oxnard, California

2000
Haus Boehl, Eisenach, Germany

GROUP EXHIBITIONS

1969
Friends of Photography, Carmel, California

1971
Geometric Progression, Santa Barbara Museum of Art,
Santa Barbara, California

1977
Santa Barbara Photography Gallery, Santa Barbara,
California

1978
Small Images, Atkinson Gallery, Santa Barbara City
College, Santa Barbara, California
Prints and Drawings (from the Museum's permanent
collection), Santa Barbara Museum of Art, Santa
Barbara, California

1979
Attitudes: Photography in the 1970's, Santa Barbara Museum
of Art, Santa Barbara, California
Arts 79 Festival, Santa Barbara Arts Council, Santa
Barbara, California
M. Shore and Son Gallery, Santa Barbara, California
The Great Outdoors, Santa Barbara Botanic Garden,
Santa Barbara, California
*Three Photographers: Ansel Adams, Brett Weston, and Robert
Werling*, Green Apple Gallery, Las Vegas, Nevada
Ojai Valley Art Center, Ojai, California

1980
At Mono Lake, traveling group exhibition with Ansel
Adams, Brett Weston, Edward Weston, Morely Baer,
Ted Orland, and others, sponsored by Friends of
the Earth
Arts 80 Festival, Santa Barbara Museum of Natural
History, Santa Barbara, California
Crocker Art Museum, Sacramento, California
Los Angeles County Natural History Museum,
Los Angeles, California
San Diego Natural History Museum, Balboa Park,
San Diego, California

1981
Hartnel College Gallery, Salinas, California
Masterworks of Photography, Keystone Gallery, Santa
Barbara, California
Arts Chateau, Butte, Montana
Landmarks in Photography, Keystone Gallery, Santa
Barbara, California
Paris Gibson Square Museum, Great Falls, Montana
Hockaday Center for the Arts, Kalispell, Montana
Arapaho College Art Gallery, Littleton, Colorado
*Photographs from the Museum's Permanent Collection,
Part I*, Santa Barbara Museum of Art, Santa
Barbara, California
Robert Werling and Todd Gray Photographs, Alexandra
Michel Gallery, Los Angeles, California
Three Landscape Photographers, Townsend Room, Santa
Barbara Public Library, Santa Barbara, California
The Downtown Gallery, Amon Carter Museum, Fort
Worth, Texas

1982
McAllen International Museum, McAllen, Texas
Hearst Art Gallery, St. Mary's College, Moraga,
California
Museum of Arts and Sciences, Macon, Georgia
Braithwaite Fine Arts Gallery, Cedar City, Utah
Humboldt Cultural Center, Eureka, California

*Photographs from the Museum's Permanent Collection, Parts
II and III*, Santa Barbara Museum of Art, Santa
Barbara, California
A Photography Show, Artists Response Gallery, Isla Vista,
California
Cabrillo Pavilion Arts Center, Santa Barbara, California
The Erotic in Art, Artists Response Gallery, Isla Vista,
California

1983
Victoria Regional Museum Association, Victoria, Texas

1985
Santa Barbara Collects, Santa Barbara Museum of Art,
Santa Barbara, California
Artwatch: A Year of Celebration, Santa Barbara Museum
of Art, Santa Barbara, California

1986
International Invitational Photography Exhibit, Centre
international d'art contemporain, Paris, France
Faces, Santa Barbara Museum of Art, Santa Barbara,
California
Homeless in Paradise, Frameworks Gallery, Santa Barbara,
California

1987
Brooks Adobe Center for the Arts, Santa Barbara,
California

1988
California Academy of Sciences, Golden Gate Park,
San Francisco, California
Fresno Metropolitan Museum, Fresno, California
*Yosemite, Then and Now—Ansel Adams, Don Worth,
John Sexton, and Robert Werling*, The Photographer's
Gallery, Palo Alto, California
Hewlett Packard, Palo Alto, California

1989
Facing the Artist, Santa Barbara Museum of Art,
Santa Barbara, California

1990
Kongresshaus, Innsbruck, Austria

1991
Friends of the River, G. Ray Hawkins Gallery,
Los Angeles, California
*Ansel Adams, Brett Weston, Edward Weston, Marion Post
Wolcott, and Robert Werling*, Foto Forum Bremen,
Bremen, Germany
Remembering Marion Post Wolcott, Santa Barbara Museum
of Art, Santa Barbara, California

1992
United States Forest Service, Mono Lake Visitor's
Center, Lee Vining, California

1993
*Warm Truths and Cool Deceits: Photographs from the
Permanent Collection*, Santa Barbara Museum of Art,
Santa Barbara, California

1996
Von oben herab, Josef Albers Museum, Bottrop, Germany

1997
American Landscapes, Galerie Faber, Vienna, Austria

2002
Draussen Vor der Tuer, Kunsthalle, Arnstadt, Germany

2004
Fotoforum International, Frankfurt am Main, Germany

PERMANENT COLLECTIONS

Ansel Adams Collection, Center for Creative
Photography, University of Arizona, Tucson, Arizona

Atkinson Gallery Permanent Collection, Santa Barbara
City College, Santa Barbara, California

Brett Weston Personal Collection, San Francisco
Museum of Modern Art, San Francisco, California

Brooks Institute of Photography Gallery Collection,
Santa Barbara, California

Carnation Company, Corporate Collection, Los Angeles,
California

Carnegie Art Museum, Oxnard, California

Imogen Cunningham Collection, Everson Museum
of Art, Syracuse, New York

International Museum of Photography and Film at
George Eastman House, Rochester, New York

Museum of Modern Art, New York, New York

National Endowment for the Arts, Washington, D.C.

Pacific Telephone, San Diego Corporate Collection,
San Diego, California

Pentax Camera Museum, Tokyo, Japan

Republic Hogg Robinson, Corporate Collection,
Cleveland, Ohio

Santa Barbara Museum of Art, Santa Barbara, California

The Huntington Library, San Marino, California

The Metropolitan Museum of Art, New York, New York

Western States Museum Permanent Collection, Brooks
Institute of Photography, Santa Barbara, California

ACKNOWLEDGMENTS

To the late Cole Weston, my good friend of more than thirty years, for sharing his recollections on Edward Weston and his personal experiences. My sincere thanks to Simone Klein for her deeply thoughtful and perceptive insights on photography, helping to put it all into perspective. My thanks to Holger Berman for his consultation and skills in realizing this project. To Michael Graser of Miro Repro for his excellent scans. To Elizabeth Scott-Graham for her fine essay about the Dunes and the Dunites. To Sherry Campbell who worked diligently at the computer to bring my images into the twenty-first century. I also thank the staff of Merrell Publishers, including Michelle Draycott, Nicola Bailey, Marion Moisy, and especially Joan Brookbank, who believed in this project from the very beginning.

INDEX

First published 2005 by Merrell Publishers Limited

Head office
42 Southwark Street
London SE1 1UN

New York office
49 West 24th Street, 8th floor
New York, NY 10010

www.merrellpublishers.com

PUBLISHER Hugh Merrell
EDITORIAL DIRECTOR Julian Honer
US DIRECTOR Joan Brookbank
SALES AND MARKETING MANAGER Kim Cope
SALES AND MARKETING EXECUTIVE Emily Sanders
MANAGING EDITOR Anthea Snow
EDITOR Sam Wythe
DESIGN MANAGER Nicola Bailey
JUNIOR DESIGNER Paul Shinn
PRODUCTION MANAGER Michelle Draycott
PRODUCTION CONTROLLER Sadie Butler

Photographs copyright © 2005 Robert Werling, except
   for p. 17 copyright © 2005 Wolfgang Bartels
   and p. 18 copyright © 2005 Edna Bullock
Text copyright © 2005 The Authors
Design and layout copyright © 2005 Merrell
   Publishers Limited
Special pre-production consultation provided by
   Holger Berman

British Library Cataloguing-in-Publication Data:
Werling, Robert
Beyond light : American landscapes
1.Landscape photography 2.North America – Pictorial
works
I.Title
779.3'67

ISBN 1 85894 296 9

DESIGNER Nicola Bailey
PROJECT MANAGER Marion Moisy
COPY EDITOR Richard Dawes
PROOF-READER Barbara Roby
INDEXER Hilary Bird

Printed and bound in Italy

FRONT JACKET
Three Brothers, Yosemite, California, 1975

BACK JACKET
Ribbon Falls, Alaska, 1981

PAGE 4
El Capitan, Yosemite, California, 1986

PAGES 8–9
Big Sur, California, 1993

PAGES 12–13
Oregon Coast, 1970